BONES OF THE EARTH

Bones of the Earth

A collection of poems
by
DONNY BARILLA

Adelaide Books
New York / Lisbon
2020

BONES OF THE EARTH
A collection of poems
By Donny Barilla

Copyright © by Donny Barilla
Cover design © 2020 Adelaide Books

Published by Adelaide Books, New York / Lisbon
adelaidebooks.org

Editor-in-Chief
Stevan V. Nikolic

All rights reserved. No part of this book may be reproduced in any manner whatsoever without written permission from the author except in the case of brief quotations embodied in critical articles and reviews.

For any information, please address Adelaide Books
at info@adelaidebooks.org
or write to:
Adelaide Books
244 Fifth Ave. Suite D27
New York, NY, 10001

ISBN: 978-1-952570-65-0

Printed in the United States of America

To,

Christine, Rob and Gwendolyn

Contents

Last Breath of Burgundy *15*

Stags and Crows *16*

Water Well *17*

Marble *18*

Edge of Winter *19*

Crush of the Treetops *20*

Passage of the Vulture *21*

Sentinels of the Woods *22*

Cedar Woods *23*

Scarlet Cloak *24*

Harvest at the Stream by the Glen *25*

Outward Slope *26*

Feeding Blackbirds *27*

Dreaming of You in the End of Autumn *28*

Empty Woods and the Golden Sand *29*

Sleeping with the Phantom   *30*
Scarlet Night   *31*
A Day in the Green Pastures   *32*
Shifting Tide   *33*
Follow the Stream   *34*
First Frost and Stiff of the Grass   *35*
These Pregnant Woods   *36*
Candlelight   *37*
Velvet Forest   *38*
Dry Branches   *39*
Walking on Cedar Chips   *43*
Hymnals   *44*
Dying Gables   *45*
Fastened in the Arms of Nightfall   *46*
Discourse in the Month of October   *47*
Sacred Breath   *48*
Pastime While Living on the Strolling Hills   *49*
Parchment Leaf   *50*
Call of the Grains   *51*
Reunion   *52*
Passages into the Woodlands of Adulthood   *53*
Parting at the Lehigh River   *54*
Season in the Another Wood   *55*

BONES OF THE EARTH

Gales of Dust *56*

Robes of Travel *57*

Breads of the Earth *58*

Last Breath *59*

Rich Soils of Antiquity *60*

Fade in the Woods at Mountain Peak *61*

Cantor *62*

Harvest *63*

I Relish These Woods *64*

Awaiting Treasures *65*

Above the Glen *66*

We Walk Through the Field and Fade *67*

Showers of Autumn *71*

Burgundy Leaves and Slip of Dew *72*

When the Path Ends *73*

Crows at Last Glance *74*

On the Edge of Slumber *75*

Return to the Mulch of Maples and Elms *76*

Soft Daylight *77*

Banquet *78*

Benediction *79*

Labor at Ocean's End *80*

Maple Treasures and Sweet Gifts *81*

Nudity of Autumn Nocturnes **82**

Early Lace **83**

Bathing in the Stream **84**

Waiting for Her Breath **85**

Searching for Her Molecules **86**

Poison Wood **87**

Morning Grass and Shaded Hues **88**

I Look for the End of Day **89**

Search **90**

Western Breath and I Sink to the Oceans Prowl **91**

Fellows Trapped **92**

Wicker Chair **93**

By the Pond **94**

Fading into the Forest **97**

Fragrance **98**

Nearest the Fallen Leaves **99**

Shelter With the Rain **100**

October Glaze **101**

Washed Through the Rhythms of the Meadow **102**

Past the Crossing Bridge **103**

October's End **104**

Winter's Advance **105**

Spirits of the Woods **106**

Passages in the Autumn Hour   *107*

In the Morning You Perish   *108*

Tender Earth   *109*

Grove   *110*

White Veils   *111*

Ivory Flank   *112*

So Near the Edge of Winter   *113*

Ancient Graves   *114*

Autumn Nudity   *115*

Travel   *116*

Travel   *117*

Empty Upon Return   *118*

Swallow of the Ocean Cove   *119*

As Frost Fell Upon the Leaves on the Forest Floor   *120*

End of Winter at the Bones of This Burial   *121*

Road's End   *122*

About the Author   *125*

Upon the breadth of this gathering of leaves,

I hear the moans of each ancestor,

eager and softly alive in the soils I love.

Last Breath of Burgundy

The slight arch of the leaves, dancing upon the maple,
cascade and gather as a wool blanket warming the earth
yet riddled in colors of red, shades of red.

This wind scours as an instrument,
the echo of a million thrashing voices pondering Autumnal ruin.

I sit forward and unbury from the pleasantries of the swabbing
pieces of parchment, soft burgundy.

I soak my tongue and mouth upon the grazing bloom of mint
and the musk of the soils of this heavy field.

With leisure, I tremble to the crooked angle of the sun
which leaps forward by brooding hour of brooding day.

I stand here for a great length and suckle the scent of the dusted leaves.

Stags and Crows

Vapors sizzled across the woodland path as I trembled forward,
I smelled the sweet fragrance of the honey, tucked well in the hive.

I paused and ducked in silence
as the stag stepped softly to the forest edge.

Crows sliced through the tree limbs and flurried forth.
I stood so gently watching the brown and whites of the deer
scurry into the shameless woods.

There sulked a fleeting bloom of each tree, heavy with Autumn.

I watched the black birds pepper the sky in glades of this forested
canvas, rooftop.

Water Well

I lean along the stone and wooden edge of the water well.
I gathered the heaviest thirst, then drank so deeply
the coolness of the crystal water slipped in ices
silently down the chapped, parchment edges of my throat.

Chilled sweats trembled across my temples and neck,
cottons of my shirt soaked swiftly the beads of sweat
which thickened my flesh in tender prisms of skin covered
rays of swift light.

With jagged stones once pressed upon my flesh,
I stood and walked through the torrents of rain tossed wind.

Marble

I flourished into dusts which carpeted and dug deeply
into the marble field.

Looking into the distance, I slept in the haze of every meadow
which bloomed chasms of light and drenched it's way
through the darkness and the richest soil.

Into the furthest hour of morning,
I rose and tug upon the moist beads which swept the endless
rows of suckling grass.

I answer to the rise of sunshine which softened and riddled
to every granule and mineral of the soil of the burrowing
glade of calmness and earth.

Edge of Winter

My shoes rest by the sliding river which crimped
with each slow glide of the soot and swooning kelp.

I gathered a fistfull of chipped and fallen acorns
as the prize of the Autumn afternoon glamoured this free
existence of orange and pink light.

I soak in the sky which carries fading blossoms of white,
opened to the lurk of this wrath of coming winter
which bleeds in nocturnes and screams in canticles.

Before the first fracture of ice and heavy falling snow,
I look to the sky as I dip through the frost of the stream.

Quietly, the measurements of this dying dash of the powders
which creep in the frozen sky, I show to the misfit of the wintery food
and carve upon the scattered tree limbs and host a flickering fire
calm upon the earth.

Crush of the Treetops

Into the outer reach of this green soaked glen,
the edges of the scattered weeds and stroking clover tugged swiftly
to the arching trees at the woodlands, softening this path with dust,
pebbled trails; I wander through this towering bloom
of majestic songs, rattling from the crush of the treetops.

Ground cover spread across the smallest spaces as I walked
barefoot and laughed at the trembling nudge of the caked earth.

Winds slaughtered with speed through the occasion of the fallen
smack of the ancient tree.

I pause and swallow the pearled dewdrops which cup
upon the quivering fern and the damp swab of the wildflower,
sweet flavors.

Into the endless width and graceful dance of the gnarled woods,
I softened and slept beneath the pine tree, here
upon the gathering nuts and swollen berries.

Passage of the Vulture

I stand as breath flickering dusts and humid vapors
in the mask of the red blushing sun.

I lean my face to the mists
of the heaviest blue skies and I witness the vulture
wrapping across the carcass and thin jousting spread
of a dying patch of fading grass.

Several deeply rooted elms fastened to the richest soils of the earth; I
soothed my feet upon the jades of the remaining pouches of grasses
which softened with every step, both ankle and toe.

Upon looking again, the vulture sank to
the furthest edge of the thinning
skyline.

I slumber in the gathered mounds of the yellow leaves.
by morning, I wake covered in the finest mist.

Sentinels of the Woods

After the smack of the rain, the puddle
widened and filled with blossoms which
surrounded as a team of sentinels.

Whistling threads of wind sharpened across the patched
wooded spread; I looked upon the films of the water.
I found washed waverings of kelp which tossed soft morning
light along every ripple of the trace of my fingers.

Leaving this oasis, I burrowed swift into the thick mass of woodlands
which weaved through the fattened girth of the falling sky
and sweet fog sweetened upon this dusted trail
which sank to the mountains edge.

I sliced my legs through these clouds and sank
upon the wooden hollow where I mumbled
a retort to the scouring winds.

Cedar Woods

I walked upon the groove of the shoreline which curved and boasted
the tossed decay of each pebble and powdered blossom
which across the cove, coiled in fragrance
of fisherman and the crooning
horns of every boat.

Thick steam rose from the quivering joust of the water.
upon clear listening, the rippled waves suckled this edge,
clamored in rock and hardened dirt.

The sky opened in a slice, torn open upon
the navy of the earliest of mornings
which spoke to the pause I gripped and the sweet fragrance I breathed.

By the moment of the bursting sun,
I walked the cedar woods and grazed upon the tremble
of this ancient home.

Scarlet Cloak

Into the walk in the depth of the scarlet cloak of night,
I soothed my way across the leaves, scattered as a fleece
In the flash of Autumn harvest.

I gathered my things and headed for a patch, empty
Of the trees as they once boasted their antiquity and rose
Well above the remaining treetops.

Nearby, the spruce flavored the aroma gliding upon the air.
I breathed until I stood and trembled with fullness.

I watched for you and you did not come.
By morning, I saddened as the flickering, sobbing ferns
Which suckle upon the tears and the dew dropped pearls.

In the northern edge of the wild trees,
hosting the reddest parchment sleeves;
I stood in the shadow and searched for you as the fields so far off;
Each swam as the waves of wind yet held no promise of you.

Harvest at the Stream by the Glen

Clovers spread by the bloods rolling across the meadow in all clear
fluids and sweet dancing blues.

The scattered wheat perched on the ledge of the stream
and gave rise to the lean of the rocks which spoke of their
coats of moss, alive in this quiet emerald glen.

Fruits of the apple tree spoke of their heavy reds which sulked
in the smoothest flesh as the tremble of her breasts,
slumbering beneath the cotton and flannel.

Disregarding her clothing and garments, she waded waist deep
in the chill of the gushing waves nearby the sunken rocks.

The sky unravelled and spoke of Autumn and her sweetest giving.
With the moan of the hunger of the dancing skies,
the wind loosened her hair and flagged walnut hues of thread and
silk;
into the muds of the fields, each step suckled the step of her foot
as grasses and onion stalks chipped each ankle and heel.

Outward Slope

I sat most still on the seat of the wicker rocking chair;
I smoothed my sight and looked upon her as she rolled
and traveled through the eggshell colored quilt.

My eyes bathed upon her nakedness and softly
the Autumnal winds tapped upon the window,
set perfectly near the sweats of her frame and bust.

With each thud of the pine cones as the settled in beds of needles,
I looked past the wealth of the widespread garden.
I smiled to the endless slope of the thick hills.

I embrace the first sting of sunlight.
Quietly, I gather my bag and set outward for the lush and lust
I find in the angle of the upward stretch.

Feeding Blackbirds

The field sat as a chess board riddled, scattered with pieces
of the swift and hungry blackbirds.

I smiled to the oak tree as branches
wavered and welcomed each flutter and pause.

I stood from the red, wooden bench and walked
through the eastern flank of the glen.

Upon reaching the heavy green wall of the forest,
I quivered to the moaning rocks as my feet
crossed and crunched upon them.

The lusts of these woods wrapped around
me with thorns and spreads
of the endless touch of ground cover.

By nightfall, I settle on the bed which lay soft against the creek.
Staying here, until my bones shook, I feed the sky, peppered
in the rise of the afternoon sun.

Dreaming of You in the End of Autumn

Clouds, once dreamed their way in pastures of swollen rains,
I settled beneath the grove of the saps where the maples
upturned each branch and gathered the droplets in smacking rhythms.

Trembling in the raspy winds and chilled
to the iced fracture, late Autumn
tugged across me in a glance while the soils of the earth
stiffened as a bed of marble.

Once my call to you, in fury I listened to the sky
which tore thin icicles across my thick
gray beard and fine walnut hair,
I stepped across the tug of the pebbled trail which slanted deeply
into the forest where I last touched you.

Into the naked trees and empty woods, I
surrendered to the slashing freeze
of the sky and all downward slant.

Gathered snowbeds wrapped across the sting of my flesh.
I hear you roam through the trees with a floundering breath,
alive these chiseled frosts.

Empty Woods and the Golden Sand

I toss, skip stones at the end of the earth
which jousted rippling waves upon the soot
from where these pebbles rooted and over a length of eons,
loosened to the shoreline and baked with the burning sun.

Burying the thick probe of my fingers and thumbs,
I sank to the kelp of you with the nakedness of my flesh and
trembling mouth.

With the quiver of moaning daylight, I
served my lips upon you and deepened into the draft
of the slapping jaunt of the sky.

Later, perched along the thick dunes of golden sand,
I watched a yellow slice of leaf wash to the watered beds offshore.

Gathering a few stones, I slipped each hand into each pocket
and roamed
the pastures of the empty woods.

Looking to the slant of the sun, I
trembled with your torso and bust, alive in each step
of the uncounted trees.

Sleeping with the Phantom

The weeping cherry tree tossed each lusty seed
as the heavy pink blossoms and petals tore through the grip
of the glen and all tangling grass.

I paused upon a mound of crimping leaves; soft breath of the rise
of the early moon slanted and carved the slivers of the fade of
moaning night.

Deepened into the bench, the swift creek sliced through the grip
of this garden and park. Here, I slumbered and waited
the eternal pause

as quiet shadows swept across the phantom of the blooming winds.

I placed the pink petal upon the palate of my tongue.

In the shatter of the morning glaze of dawn,
I surrendered to the shift
of the trickling dancing water and drank deep as I stood
and walked the tread of the earth and scurried home.

Scarlet Night

Steps upon the tread of the thick scarlet trim
where mosses stroked the trunks of the vine covered trees,
I smiled to the wrapping branches which cluttered through
the stroke of this wild treetops; I sank
and paused by the spread of endless grazing rocks.

Here, the cloak of nightfall deepens and darkens within
as I coat the cottons of my shirt
with trembling sweats coating the dampness of these dark woods.

With the flicker of early sunshine,
I stand and deepen through the emerald glades which gloat, glisten
across the pastures of the rising quilt of the earth.

A Day in the Green Pastures

Green pastures slept silently with tangled ribboned clouds
melting upon the blue canvas and page.

With each sweet loft of scents of the honey hive,
I carved my path through the tender mint.

I lean along the trunk of the red maple which yearned
for the creams of the yellow sun, dancing tides and rhythms
stirred and I slumbered through the approach of night.

Into the endless flicker of the endless blades of weeds
and the soft wrangle of the fields,

I stroked the wavering press of wind which soothed me
into the heavy groan; I speak with the soils full of mineral,
mulch and marrow.

Shifting Tide

Deep in the clutch of frosted Autumn,
I walk the grove and frequent the aromas of the quiet freeze
which snaps beneath the step of my leather boots.

With the flood of the icy creek, swift sauntering leaves
speak of their regal grooming wash on the spread of the open waters.

I tremble beneath the wools which gather the white petals.

Softly, the sky opens to a gush of flickering snow showers;
I am here in these dashing flakes of perfect white.

Follow the Stream

The chipped and shaved pine cones imbedded and soothed
along the needles of the every evergreen sloping and jousting
across the climb of the mountain stretch.

Sweet scents of these fragrant woods dashed across the winds
as they wrapped across me in vanishing cloaks of approaching Winter.

I felt the pulse of the trickling spring, gushing water fed the mountain
descent and fattened to the stream, slithering across the deep meadow,
alive with the spread of leaves soft in every color and hue.

I shook the moisture and dewdrops from the chill
of my shoulder, neck
and glisten of my soaked, thin hair.

Looking to the fibers of the eggshell white scurry of the sky,
again, I walked into the growth of the widespread woodlands.

Above me, the blackbirds threshed the winds and carved their way
upon the lift of the Autumn breath.

First Frost and Stiff of the Grass

Harvests patterned these leaves across the
glen: the elm, the maple, red maple,
the willow and the sycamore.

I felt the dusts of this sweet drenched
October dance with perfect gesture
wildly across the snap of the stiffened grass.

Winds blitzed across the mounds of various colored leaves.

I soaked in every stitch and fiber which
rested, glazed in the frosts
of the first ices of the shaking meadow by branch and swooning
purr of the silent grass.

With wind slashing across the sting of my
flesh, I spoke to the moaning
burrow where the bones of my ancestors
rival at the edge of every Autumn.

These Pregnant Woods

Soft, crisp rains chiseled across the open gulf of the sky
as the distant forest of hills welcomed each thread of fog,
the scurry of pressing mists.

I walked into the reach of the pregnant woods.

Every splash of moss and quiver of the fern leaf, floundered
across the dampness of the rattling drops of water, fallen
from the canvas swiftly bowing across the sky, hushed
to the thinning leaf.

To the sweet charms of the spread of the woods,
I surrendered in the arms of this lush,
loafing breath which trembled
across the surface of the heavy leaf.

In a moment, a branch snaps and falls upon
the edge of my stride and toe
of my burrowing foot.

Candlelight

You shook upon this ocean, quiver of this down feathered bed.

Pale apricot hues stretched along these marrow filled bones
and I glazed you sweetly in creams and solutions.

A moment past, I watched the skylight flicker in tongues of the candle
which groomed and paused upon you with warmth of your
shadowed breasts, washing upon me in ribbons of the evening harvest,
dashes of the silver light.

Your flesh spread as a quilt and gathered each thash of warmth.

Softly, I ached upon the thick heat, burn of this cove which fastened
to the swoon of your trembling thighs which spoke to the flesh
which held swift in perfect angles and touch.

Velvet Forest

I walk upon the velvet floor of the forest;
sweet song of the mourning dove carries through the gales;
softness of the emerald greens stroke each
tree, stone and fallen branch.

Laughter of the crashing, crackling branches echo across the woods.

I lay upon the carpet of the woodlands and strengthen
myself to a silent sleep as the first leaf of Autumn
gently falls on the edge of my shoulder.

I awaken through the thick of night and step upon the pouch
of the onion grass and ducked beneath each shoot of bamboo.

With the tongues of the rise of morning,
I weaken on the glaze of the Autumn
earth which soaks my denim and speak to me of return.

Dry Branches

I gather the dry, dead branches and fallen twigs.
Smoke rises across the breadth of the slender field.

Looking to the west, I witness the pinks and purples
of the surrendering sun.

I feel you breath as the warmth crosses my face and lathers
pale sunshine across my neck as it tugs my full, walnut colored hair.

I speak to you of each tangle and crimp of each resting, falling leaf.

Walking on Cedar Chips

I knelt to the scatter of the grape hyacinth
which housed upon the floor of the soft wood.

With the palm and grip of my hand, I loosened a quivering petal,
with twitch and waver, a gust of wind lofted
this prism of beauty to the swollen sky.

Walking home,
I stepped on the path, alive in the fullness of the cedar chips.

Opened and full, these lungs assembled
the aromas of the breeze of the forest.

I reached camp and listened to the laughter of the spiny creek.

In the slumber of night, I dreamed of lavenders and purple vines.

Hymnals

The sun rose with chariots flashing across the yellow stretch.

I heard the mumbling winds which holstered each groove and valley;
this tremble of a heavy, the heaviest choir, danced across me
as the grass of the valley angled and delicately sang of triumph.

I swam through the floods of this music and sat restful
upon the burn of the flat, stretching stone.

Dying Gables

Dusts roamed the dying earth and coiled across leaves.

I listen to the treasures of this endless citadel of trees,
alive in the gables of tower and stretch of gnarled, crackling branches.

My feet stepped modest along the vein of threaded grass.

Silent, I looked above and watch the merlot tossing leaf
which landed upon the scurry of each leaf, tender, the dance
of the parched cup and seed bury within the grave of the earth.

Looking, from east to west of the horizon,
I felt and witnessed the dash
of the first frost which crunches every stitch of humble life.

Fastened in the Arms of Nightfall

I fell to the meadow, burrowed across
the earth and lathered each weed and emerald grass
in the scattered blush of my ashes.

The fragrance of the tumbling leaves wrapped across her sinewy legs
which levelled the soils and dusts as an angled broom.

I speak to her of the song of the blackbird
and the approach of the soothing rain.

Mulch, lining the trees of the groaning woods, spoke of my glazes
well beneath the heavy gloss of the moist sky.

I trembled and shook the patterned soot from my flesh;
quiet desperation saddled the toss of my face and cottons of my
clothing.

I answer the dashing questions of disrobing each patch of flesh
as the mourning nightfall lulled upon my moaning bones.

You walk across me and I am soothed to the quilt of each step.

Discourse in the Month of October

These wheat fields wavered to the breath of the end of Summer
which clashed against the haze the peach and purple skies,
dancing upon the thrashing of each loosened seed, landing upon the moist
soil which dripped in fertility.

Nearby, the slice of the creek fumbled in bashful tolerance
as the pebbles and smaller rocks flickered light of the passing
evening. I look to the west and watch the fields lull the cool
Autumn sky.

By the end of this rapture of fresh water and lusty
openings which carve against the approaching rain,
I fell to the spreading acres of moss across the forest floor
and with soft breath and rhythms, I slumber and meet each
pellet of rain in all it's discourse.

Sacred Breath

I motioned my arms to the distant sun
which unravelled and sank beneath the thinnest edge
of the horizon and offered a gushing blaze of the darkest
navies and the soft flame of the sliced apricot.

Within each second of these pulsing moments of sacred
breath called nocturnes, I stand upon the
ledge which rose to a summit
and bathed me in nakedness.

This breast of the swelling touch of the full moon
cast showers of an eager fragrance which swelled to me in warmth
and touch the sauces of the torrent and it's approaching dew.

Pastime While Living on the Strolling Hills

The grooming winds spread through the arms and branches
of the sweet red maple; I watch the fog slither apart
along each reach of quivering wooden limbs.

I strode the hills of Pennsylvania as the clouds sank beneath me.

I trembled through the scattering of the pine tree.
So near, the creek gushed from the bulbous rocks as gently
I drank and felt the razors of the ice suckle upon my throat.

Resting upon the pinecones and weathered needles, I sank
into the soft beds of her as the distant mountains fed
the meadows of the valley as the breast of the warming earth
coiled in each sinking cloud.

I call to you in a whisper as the dewdrops of your nook and cove
dripped and sauntered upon my lips.

Parchment Leaf

Shavings of the ancient oak shuffled and gathered
upon the spread of the soil and mulch which took
to the bloom of the swift sky.

A single shred of parchment once loosened, tangled
upon the wools of my sweater and edged to my jacket
as the hidden words moaned for the tempest
storming across the horizon which lulled blackness
through the breadth of these crippled Summer winds.

On the peak of Autumn, these leaves of yellow and red
surrendered to the softness where laughter lost upon
the harvest dance.

I walked the edge of the woods which stood painted as a canvas
and trembled each breath along the flesh of me, apples
and the juice of the fig cascading in relishing swallows.

In a moment, the harvest caved and slipped through the fingers
as the enchantment of creams of the creek slipped
across my ankle and foot.

Call of the Grains

The velveteen cloaked the night's sky as each
Whistle threshing through the forest and all garments
Which lay upon the breadth of the earth in cottons and gauze,
Soaked me in the gluttony of these pastures so near.

Soft muds puckered the wedge of my boots as I
Remove my shirt and vest and offer my nakedness
To the needling rains.

Well into the deep of night, I
Tossed the humidity of my breath as the flesh of me
Chapped as the ice of a forgotten season.

I follow the trace of the moon and swelled to the harvest
Of the grains which call to me in meadow and field.

Reunion

Trampling sticks and snap of the bone which chants echoes
well beneath the earth, I witness the fever of the fog
and thick swab of this morning mist; I soon will disappear
into the dampness of the slithering soils which brood upon me;
quiet now, I soften to each stone and grave.

I feel your hair as the wind through my hair.
I sleep upon you as the mosses and onion weeds suckle me.

I withdraw to the tumbling breath of the mountainside;
thin, pale clouds wrestle across the stillness of my once, blood
filled flesh.

I return to you and soften with each passing step.

Passages into the Woodlands of Adulthood

The children climbed, shook the branches on the treetops
which leaned and angled to the prism of the sun.

After smiling to the youth,
I left for the source of the sweet mountain spring.

With my body filled with the juice of the patient earth,
I threaded through valleys and searched for the forbidden woods.

Across the dip of the valley,
I heard the perfect echo streaming through the tender current of air.

Parting at the Lehigh River

As she pushed into the slow current of the great river,
I fastened in witness to the nakedness she sauntered;
quietly, the full gush washed upon her as the cool water
melded her to the soft of the riverbed.

Upon return, her deep rooted chestnut hair
slithered in blacks across her shoulders and back.

I kissed her on the pale flesh of her breasts
and returned to the foam of the current from which I came.

Season in the Another Wood

Shreds of the crimped leaves which crimp
to shreds and toss to the swift wind, carries each fiber
to land upon the flesh of our naked body.

Sweet gems of the nearest edge of the forest
lulls each sway and tug of each molecule
and suckles them into the breads of the earth.

I walk upon you as the moist and most fertile soil
croons and saunters across me with scents which once blossomed
well into the pause of the sun and dripped tossing mint.

I burrow next to the endless jousting trees.
with the slash of the skyline, I stormed along the soft
breasts which wrap against the sweet verbs of the deep.

Gales of Dust

I surf upon the flicker of the brown, tan and pale green grass.

This wash of the meadow soothes with soft touch
as I deepen into the moisture of the earth; I moan to the dripping fog
which melds to me in cakes and precious tortes.

The pebbles which rub along the nakedness of my flesh
swoon me to the tremble of hurried nightfall.

The burgundy leaves speak of sweet winds which carry my sweat, dew
and sweep of the molecules into the heavy voices of each
crack and shuffle of the triumphant trees.

I feel the bloods of my bones as the fever of this cloaked
sweep of the dome of the heaven saunters upon me.
the soils deepened within the ground where I sleep and soften.

When the wind fractures across the steep of the mountain,
I loosen and travel to you in gales of dust.

Robes of Travel

Green felt strapped to the mound, sleek hill of boulders.
Floods of the emerald carpet, when passed
the summit, carved through
the garments of the wooded trail.

The aromas tossed from the black mulch,
threading across the base and edge of each tender sap
of each tender tree; this musk bloomed across the mountainside
and nestled into the fullness of my mouth and lungs.

At the end where the shadows stretch and the mists and vapors
rub the endless carving edge, I loosen upon the westward winds
and soak among the valley, meadow and countryside which offers
me this lusty earth for pause and for the robes of travel.

Breads of the Earth

Autumn cottons which spread and shuffled across the meadow
where I met you, packed into the moans of the trembling
wind which caressed across the valley, pale green in all it's lusty
crimp where the phantoms of October lurked into coves of sweet
flavors and the breath of dissolution.

I stood upon the soft soils of the meadow where I find, gather you
into the wash of my mouth.

I press to the heavy pattering rain.
with each crackle of your bones and grooved tastes
flickering in my mouth, tongue,
I suckled the fog which undressed from the flesh of you.

I rise with the sting of my humid breath and quietly
I wade into the coated breads of the earth.

Last Breath

The paleness of your flesh suckles upon the moisture
which softens and grooves the edges of your perfect
rib and your perfect sloping waist.

I further my walk across the trim path, leading
into the swelling humid woodlands.

I felt the gravity of the thinnest clouds as they dripped
and fell across each trembling treetop and coated
me in an endless flush of dancing wind.

Upon reaching the furthest nook of the center of the woods,
I lean against the majestic reach of the pierce, the maple
sings with each current and dazzles the passing breath of the wind.

Once more, I think of her and burrow into the deep of the forest
so alive in glazes.

Rich Soils of Antiquity

I followed the chipped white fence which trimmed the stretch of the soft
speech of the meadow, quivering jade.

Upon following the wooden brackets and posts held
deeply into the earth, I met the tender madness of the forest
which shed hues of red, yellow and shades of brown as my
feet sulked into the earth, speaking of rich soils of antiquity.

I soured to the moisture and humidity of the early grip of Autumn.

Reaching the cove of the center of the woods,
thousands of leaves rest as a scattering of pages and parchment.

After a moment of silence, I lost my way.

Fade in the Woods at Mountain Peak

My feet scurried along the edge of the creek;
silence crushed across me as the warmth of the first pinch
of the cloak of night sliced along this fragment of Autumn,
swiftly alive in the garment of each shaving of woods.

Reaching the peak of the trembling sauces of pond and scattered puddles,
I drank and lay across the moss coated stones and slabs of rock.

Tenderly, I fade among the jaunt of the perfect breeze
which lulled me with the breath of the suckling root and swab of the soil.

Cantor

Beneath the crusts of the earth, wrapped from root to scents
of drifting aromas of well tossed mulch,
I threaded my path through the lining of the red maple,
sweetly swaying to the calm tremor of leaf and supple twig.

Bleeding into the fade of the pinks and indigos of this
approach of the night's glaze, alive with the softest dew,

I listen to the moan of the crackling trees which sang of the cantor
of the perfect glances of these sap soaked woodlands.

Tender upon the soft ground, I loosen into nakedness and shift
into the hush of the most rich, suckling Autumn.

Harvest

Tugging rich scents of the pregnant forest floor,
I sweat upon the lips of her as each breath of harvesting life
swoons in a flash to the tossing October sky;
pinks and purples blend with the carve of the bones,
I soothe with the marrow upon her heavy breasts.

She disrobes, sulks in forgotten fleeces with the gathering breeze.
As I lift to the dusts which toss and return upon
the sleek slab of the mountain creek, she touches me in the veils
of the quiet pauses of the stretch of the earth.

In the last touch of my hand upon the sweat of her temple,
neck, breast and shoulder, I burrow into the softness.

I Relish These Woods

I walk across the trim grasses and gather
raindrops upon my cottons and denim.
Surrounded, the warm air dashes and reflects across me.

To the east with the rise of the sun, I step
upon this glaze of meadow and grass.
I covet this place with the smooth relic
and fondling kelp of the curve
of the creek.

In the oldest moment of my youth, I slowly fade into the restless
rattle of these ancient trees.

I surrender to the sky and relish each nook and cove of every
musk of timber and sting of the mints
which soon will gather around me.

Awaiting Treasures

As I rest with the soils of the meadow,
well into the depth of the valley, I moan
with the spread of the Autumn
leaves.

With laughter of the dimly lit branches and flickering buds,
worn and ready to sleep in the glen,
I suckle the moisture on each pat of dew.

With the sweet cove of my hollow bones,
I quake to the rapture of the blossoming reach
of the end of the Autumn groove, prowl.

At the end of the peach thickened sky,
winds of this last thread of warmth sweep across me.

Here, within the shroud of dust, dirt and clay, I sleep
as I wait for your flesh to tremble next to me.

Above the Glen

The breads of you quiver as the breasts which motion
with the fullness of this flesh, filled with thick creams.

I reach the summit upon this mountain peak.
I cast a gaze and witness the spread of the endless green glen

which edges to the thin mist of the horizon.

In the fracture of a moment, I enter the dance of Autumn leaves
as the branches crackle and moan with each smack of timber
and shred of the loosest bark.

I covet you in each shadow and scent of the softest powders.

We Walk Through the Field and Fade

With an early coat of powdery November mounds,
snows tremble, dance across the stiffness of the sweet fields.

In precision, the next moment of late Autumn casts
silk muds through the edge of my boot and the thread

Of my denim cuff. Skies and cotton clouds above slice and sever,
casting a flicker of sunlight as the snow piles suckle upon the earth.

I watch the softest of your steps as you walk into the gluttony
of the thick fogs which wrap you in the soak and tremor;
alive this endless fade crumbles across you in mist.

I surrender myself to the richness of the fat of the earth and soil.

I covet the rapture of the treads of each passing flake.

*Wandering in search of her,
I speak with the bones of each ancestor.*

Showers of Autumn

Across the fields of the Pennsylvania golden dash,
the sun pampers and coddles every taste: wheat, rye, maize,
soy and the soft caked mud of the earth which bakes against me.

Rain of the heaviest drop fondles to the edge of my lips.

I walk through the sweet scented honey and tug upon
the rooted deep of the onion root which moves my dampness
to the quaking smash of this maddened thunder.

Gales of the ash gray sky, spread along the cool fevers of the meadow
in which I gently stand.

Burgundy Leaves and Slip of Dew

I surround myself in the waters of the sky;
I feel the slapping pound of the welcoming glazes
of the end of Summer, deepened into the scattered green buds
and wave of the limes of grass.

The sky cast a last spread of warmth as the burgundy leaves,
full upon the red maple, cupped and soaked sweet rain which
arrived upon the passage through the threshold of gentle harvest.

I open myself to the capped tremble of the slicing stream
which scurried through the garden, meadow and entered
the fullness of the woods,
stanced as the breadth of the castle, mansion and keep.

Searching for passage, I follow the clutter and goan of the brook
as my feet losses their way and I savor, fall to the depth
of the mounded gathering of leaves which fondle the drip
my flesh; I sulk to the leaves and trickle of each slip of dew.

When the Path Ends

Into the wealth of the spread of the glen, stroked and lined
with the thick timber of the woods,
I soaked my trembling eyes to every piece of pine and spear of grass.

To the farthest distance of the bulge and reach of the mountains,
I gathered my things, my staff and walked with soft steps
to the trail which marks each breach of these sinking clouds,
alive in the dim light of Autumn.

I enter the surmounting trickle and soothing float of fog;
I witness the fade of my chalk white flesh.

Pines and spruces lather the beds of the forests earth.
Well into the hollow of the cove, circed in trees which stab to heaven's roof,
I quiver and shake as I lose my way.

Crows at Last Glance

I invoke the spread and grace of the oakwood.
I tangle upon the fibers of the roots which suckle the moisture
Of the floods of the earth.

In a dash, the crow patterns to the shifting motions of the sky.
I breath the aromas as the heavy grays of clouds surmount.

With the slips and jousting beads which groove into the endless
Leagues of the soil, I return to the most eager trembling branch.

With the loosening of my flesh, I fed the shave of the trunk,
The scattered acorns tapping the emeralds of moss.

With a last glance, I grovel to the crows, now peppering
The darkening sky.

On the Edge of Slumber

Heavy moisture bloomed sour across the fragrance of the earth.

I stooped to the bark of the fallen log which
creaked and moaned to the marrow beneath the pebbles
and clay beds of the pasture where I rest.

You return to me in the quivering scents of the hyacinth,
passing sweetly along the flesh of my bust and torso.

Gently, I fondle these memories in the cupped leathers
of my palms.

Gently, I rise most humid as the rains tap against my neck.
falling to a slumber, once more, I reach my fingers and touch
the shadowed curves of your breasts.

Return to the Mulch of Maples and Elms

Within the shadow of the wood, songs reached the relish and molds
of each sway of each towering treetop, suspended as a canvas
of emeralds and jades.

With the snap of a fallen branch, beneath the press of my foot,
I stopped and watched the creek slice downward as I recall
the opened dash of the bolder resting on the plateau.

I tremble with the chill and reaching winds
which speak of this loosening
bed, coddled in the arms of Autumn.

I bathed, knee deep, walking through the painted glaze of the leaves
which aspire to pat and return as the mulch, feeding the distant
maples and elms.

Again, I kneel to the threads of an icy wash and drink.
This forest suckles me and I loosen upon each fade of grass.

Soft Daylight

The abdomen, slick with trembling dew, awoke to glamor
of the earliest wash of sun; I tasted the flavors of the meadow
and the breath of the October breeze.

I touched the breasts of her which wrangled across me,
alive in the flavors of the harvest.

I paused at the fluids of the coursing stream and drank once
as I arrived in the depth of channel and stroking kelp.

I walk in the glazes of the spiny path and tempt my burrowing chill
to the floods of each wet, suckling leaf.

With adhesion to the sulk of the sinking sky, floods of clouds,
groomed me in age and groan of my flesh
which dashes to floundering
shout of soft daylight.

Banquet

Crossing the pasture and the clever rise of the towering mountain
wore a cloak which danced and threaded: reds, tans, browns, pale yellow
and the deepest shade of burgundy.

The scent of beautiful death captured upon the ground
gathered itself and took flight to the quaking winds.

Standing alone, I placed an apple in the palm of my hand;
I sank my teeth and suckled the flesh along the moisture of my tongue.

Slowly, the earth chilled and stiffened as I heard the snap of each jade patch
of grass in the retreat of this meadow.

Entering the glazes of this wooded mountain clinging to the tossing
cotton of the drifting sky, tapping upon the chiseled peak;
I rest in this empty wood and sleep upon the soft banquet of the earth.

Benediction

I walk casually through the countryside, gingerly upon the rocks
and the stones as they lay scattered.

Into the fracture of morning, the fires of pink and red
fastened from the eastern horizon and spread, telling tales
of the baptism of the early hues of benediction.

Feeling my flesh greet the soft mists as I gather within the settling fog,
carpets of the mask here upon the soil suckle me in this soothing cup
of muds and grass clippings.

Further into the smack of daylight, I gather a covenant with stroking
lusts as each thrash of quivering wheat brooms across me.

Walking across the endless field, I fade through the sunken clouds
and surrender to the wet soils as I tremble into the heavy scarlet of
night.

Labor at Ocean's End

I linger above the treads of the surface as I speak in eager
dance and forbidden tongues.

I humbly ask, "enter me in these silk fogs which caress
the reflection of the supple moon which slithers each molecule
of wash and brine."

I glance across the cove of this groove of the bay.
I swab through the thinning glaze across the water,
edges of the pine grove which summons me.

Well into the fade of the random gulls which lust
after fish and the groom of the rising breath across the water
and the water's deep.

With a last gust of wind, I loosen and
fade to the wetlands and inlet.

Lifting to the mountain crest, I spread
in eager groves and icy caves
which rest as the fog horns call upon me to surrender
to the salted moans of the fumbling croon
as she suckles upon the depth
of the clever pasture where the wheat of
her thighs roam the open sea.

Maple Treasures and Sweet Gifts

Bloods of the maple tree soothed each shred of bark,
softly I breathed the syrups and fastened to you
as you place the small, supple chill of your hands
tenderly upon my resting thigh and and the surmounting warmth
tender upon my groin.

I ask the heat of the dissipation of the sun, trembling in pinks
which lather the edge of the sky.

I loosen the softness of your cotton garments and feed the burrow
of this fading light as gentle leaves gather and collect.

Now, in the passions of night, I retreat to the pale softness
of your abdomen and the alabaster white of your breasts.

The sauces of these patterns which engulf upon each shaking
branch in which I gaze to the emptiness of the trembling woods.

Well in the depth of the forest grove, I place a staff from the maple
and I raise my voice to the scowling blaze of the Autumn blush.

With you, in a moment, I leave this realm and drink upon the syrups
and sweet taste of the governing dewdrops.

Nudity of Autumn Nocturnes

Wind swam through the grass and spoke of nocturnes
which hummed like a choir and sent soft glances
from each naked tree as the branches trembled.

Now, well into the deep of Autumn, I sat upon
the fallen log which granted each frozen moss, spread
across the dead, silent bark.

At the pinnacle of morning, I rose and in this glazed, last
moment of Autumn and softly the sun breached the trim
horizon of the east and I chased the gushing silvers
of the gluttonous moon.

Early Lace

Early, the snowstorm gathered as a pattern of lace
And upon the naked hill, settled as a
fleece, so deserving of the earth.

In a silent pause, I felt the growth of the hillside
Sink in the first motionless bed of white.

I mourn for the dead harvest of Autumn
as the garments of her flesh
Rest upon my wooden floor, gathered near the wood stove

Which cast collections upon the flickering
light, trembling and dancing
Across the nakedness of the warmth of her flesh.

I turn and face the slicing winds as they scurried and tossed
Each flake into a haze, sweating as dew across the chill of my
Slightly warmer flesh.

Steering, heading home, I lost my way
and sat soft and iced to the freeze
Of this tread.

In the dash of morning, I fade to the breach of morning light.

Bathing in the Stream

I unravelled from the clothing which soaked each trickle of sweat.
tenderly, the fullness of my walnut colored hair clung to the temples
which perched each strand of silk.

With the passions of your grooming growth, I embraced you
and softened this trembling, weary flesh upon yours.

Severed clouds of ash gray passed the moist rains so heavy
upon the closeness of the stream.

With you, we wade into the water and held the brim,
waist deep and I fastened to the water and the fading burn
eager upon your shoulders.

Moments later, an elm leaf slick, travels across the swimming growth
of the greenest stream, so filled with kelp.

I grab the leaf in my hand and slowly, I walk home.

Waiting for Her Breath

I ran the tips of my fingers across her breasts
as waving arms of the willow tree.
Warm wind crossed across my face
as once, earlier, the bleeding sun coated me in leathers.

Trickling, small, the creek passed as the minerals of the soil bed
dribbled in sauces and moistened each patch of emerald grass
and fed the rise of the onion sprout.

I sat and leaned against the willow as my feet lanced every
slice of the coolest waters which bloomed upon me.

Each passing rivet loosened the breath of me.
Each gust of this loafing breeze threaded through my full, dark,
brown hair.

I stood and walked through the tangled, heavy field and smiled
to the warm breath slithering upon my ears and face.

Looking across my burning shoulders, the willow tree thickened,
deeply upon it's
haunches and swelled quiet the buds and branches.

I crossed the threshold of the sweet air of jasmine which quivered
to the side of her home.

In the loosening tide of clothing and garments, I surrendered to
her sultry breath
which wrangled me in rhythms.

Searching for Her Molecules

I rest upon the earth and wait for the summoning of the heavy
quilt of nightfall which covers me in scents of the fruited trees,
fall of the chipped pinecone and lulling aromas where these fields
flicker upon me in every sensation.

I burrow my fingers and thumbs into the earth as I search for the
molecules
of her; I dig for the threads of her fading hair and arrive to this
dark green patch of fading flesh.

Through this meadow, I cleave the highest thicket
and summon my gasp upon the heavy winds.

I walk to the thin passage through the woods which relish and
hold me
as each strand of life strikes me in needles and thorns
swelling across the path while I lather myself in the absence of her
fullness and pale, soft skin.

Poison Wood

The dirt pass to the wide and heavy woods
begged for me, begged for my feet and these thick brown boots.

The sycamore trees triumphed as an arch, an entrance into
this wilderness thickly, warmly begging for the moisture of my flesh
and the sweats trembling from each nook and cove.

Upon arrival, I swim through the deep.
Scattered ponds, lathered in the slowest motions of the heaviest fog,
crawl upon the stance of my body and curl to my flesh.

In the eternal search for the passages and dripping acres of life,
I fade with the trembling snap of empty creeks and murk filled waters
which leave me swollen by the moaning press of the poison wood.

Morning Grass and Shaded Hues

The cloud filled sky opened and gifted the thick, heat filled orb
which flashed warmth to the glazes of the morning gasp
of air, floods rose each slaughtered blade of lime grass
and searched the fields for depresses of moisture, awaiting
the slab of the sloping hill, calmly.

I Look for the End of Day

At the end of day with slivers of the bent shadow of the fade
beneath the slender horizon, I tremble upon the depress
of the mud soaked earth.

From the distant grove of the fleshed, full apple trees, I
motioned my way to the serpentine, slither of the creek.

I drank from the cup of my hands and the crisp juices,
alive in the richest of mineral water, slid
down the dry edges of my throat.

With patience and the dark scarlet cloak which swabs across my
tender, quivering thighs, I sank well into the cool floods of the banks
and I wade to the ankles, I spirit into the waters.

I stand cleverly and walk to the floods in the high tumble
gushing downward past trees and moan of the holly bush.

By morning, I slumber beneath the cloak of a gathering of maples
which cast full shadows and wash me in sweet breezes.

Softly, I dissipate to the silence of the
dashing descension of each flicker
of each particle of breath.

Search

Leaves tossed with the crackling of branches;
I hear the whipping tones,
soothing notes of the chime which echoes
and flourishes through the woods.

The tapping brisk raindrops follow the
roots and discourse of the spoken
vowels and consonants.

Eagerly, I step upon the furthest burrow of the bones sunk to
the deepest swallow where my tender flesh
murmurs and waits in this patient
groove of the softest mesh where the sky flooded upon and the
tangled root whispers of continuity of flesh and dust.

Now, past the stove of the Summer's reach, I enter the cove.

I walk the endless graves of the earth as each earth suckles
as a grave and I coil upon the rib of Adam.

With sinking legs and aching waist, the trembling soft curves
of the meadow speaks so inviting.

Western Breath and I Sink to the Oceans Prowl

She lay silent and sacred in the nakedness of the shadow
of this sky, so filled with trembling barleys.

The slight perfections of her flickering hair took to the winds
which tossed each silk lock upon her pale, alabaster shoulders.

From the western breath cast the granules of sands;
the chill of her empty mouth and crimp of each lip
murmurs to the slither of this vacancy.

I reach to the freeze of her flesh and sweet fragrances
of the nearby mint patch which hovers as an incense tumbling
gently across the sands of the foam spread bloods;
I covet each as rituals into the marble sky.

Fellows Trapped

The road lay thick with ice as the depth
of October suckles the passage
and cripples the branches of maple trees,
now frozen to the slashing gust
of trembling winds.

I feel the frosted flesh which keeps trapped in silence and layers
the sting to the marrow as the flesh loosens and the sweet words
of each predecessor halts upon the quiver of the frozen tongue.

I return to the rock strewn road and flee beneath the marble sky
as I witness each sliver of the clouds and I mumble to the
fresh prism of this fondling sweet descension.

In the end of this road, I slip into the
caverns pouched upon the silence
of the passage end.

With fangs of needles, I slipped through
each sting as I coddled the fire
swelled in the pebble strewn earth.

I hear the echoes of my kin and welcome
in the scurry of fellowship.

Wicker Chair

I sit gently upon the curve of the wicker chair, chipped
and shaved, now loosened to the wooden bones which rest beneath.

Well past the deceased waves of the Summer heat,
I now serve the scuffle of each leaf drifting to this Autumn fragrance.

This roaming scatter of colored, crimping dusts
settle among the tender beds of an October dress,
quiet and full with passage, in a moment, dead and eager for the
mulch of a most distant Spring.

The tall spears of the pine tree quicken to the fury of the sweetest
sky.

I stand and walk to the furthest edge of the woods.
Upon return, the dancing leaves hush across the forest floor.

By the Pond

The green face of the lurking, deep of the pond
wavered each strand of kelp and tangled the heel of each foot.

A lone leaf of the hickory drifted across this
film, open as an arena to the loosened grip of each tree,
settled by the bank of the settled wash.

Soon, I whispered to the fast breeze of the sky and all it's dome.

I hear each drift of each falling leaf.
I quiver beneath the wools as the sky opened and pressed
rain upon me.

In the swelling tapping waters which
gripped and retreated the waves of kelp, I followed the track
of the Autumn sky and fleshed
myself in the greens and navies of the pond.

Well into October, I loosen the bones of the earth.
In a moment, I taste the floods of the leaves,
pounded to the mulch of a most distant Spring.

Fading into the Forest

Swollen waves caress the shore by the pebbles of the lake;
soft, the skies curl and pat upon the narrow docks.

I remove myself from the stitches and hems of these clothes
which once warmed my flesh in the Autumn glazes of the falling
gales.

Wading through the shave of the sweet waters,
I explore the traces and suckling sheaves of ripples
with the nakedness of my pale flesh.

After the jaunt, I walk upon the sands and stones which carved
edges and scratches of my leathery feet.

Gingerly, the wind wash across me and I listen to the deepest
hum of the foghorn and caress of the waves upon the wooden
docks.

Tenderly, I deepen into the pine woods which howl
every crack of every branch as I fade into the needled floor
of the trembling forest, alive at the peak of dawn.

Fragrance

Upon walking through the woods,
walking to the end, edge of the woods,
I lean to the emerald grass and gatherings of sweet wild flowers,
I suckle upon the crisp dressing of the cooler winds
of the October sky and gently I step to the aimless fields.

With clever rains soothing the paleness of my flesh,
I breath the pollens and seeds of the bursting pods.

I saunter slow as the silence of the trembling dome of the sky,
reaches every flicker of grass and the earth soaks the steps
of my feet, these leather boots.

I peer to the rise of the distant mountain peak.
Upon arrival, I drink the water which soothes you into the patch
of the dryness of my throat.

I gather you into the thick, dredge of my palms and softly
I recall the fragrances of your once naked body.

As the air thins, I tremble forth and sulk across the mountain
deep.

Nearest the Fallen Leaves

As clouds thinned and fell upon the meadow,
strewn as the spread of cotton, I walked with the dip of my
trembling feet and breathed the scent of patches of mint.

Standing fresh to the sky, well upon the shroud of the openness
of the majestic oak, I tossed myself upon the shaving bark
and fell to a silent slumber.

In the dashing hours of Autumn, I deepen to the soils of the earth.

Shelter With the Rain

I slip my fingers across the paints of her lips
as the humid breath of her cascaded across with the warmth
which flushed and burrowed within me.

Resting the angles of my face softly upon the shadows and paleness
of her trembling breasts, I shake upon the dark of the wooden room.

In the hurry of a moment,
I reached and touched each quiver of each stalk of wheat.

The beads of dew dispersed upon the dance of my lips
as the blossom of the moon danced through the bay window.

In the deepest hour of night,
I slept upon her as rains tapped every nook of the house.

October Glaze

The path curved across the slender edge of the mountain,
reaching upon the summit which stretched narrowly
through the scarce grooming of the spruce, calm and full of retort
to the gush of sweeping winds.

Stopping upon the drench of the clearest spring, I
fasten to the bed of fallen needles and deeply I drank.

By the sink of the blushing clouds which deepen to the valley,
spread aimless with meadow and pasture,
I coiled and fell to the slumber of this fresh October glaze.

Washed Through the Rhythms of the Meadow

Wind slashed in rhythms across the scattering of the maples
as each leaf loosened to the sky, fell upon the dampness
of the field which rested in lime colored grass and the spread
of burgundy.

I waded through the dress of the calmness,
after the torrents and clamor
of the gusts of wind.

Now, I look to the dome of the velvet night.
I slip through the dew laden meadow as shoots of the onion grass
slithers across my ankles and the quenching droplets
soaking into the threads of these wet denim jeans.

The trail burrowed through the edge of the narrow woods.
The death of the leaves and parched saunter of the pine
and each fallen needle caked upon the press of my boots
which deepen upon the thick, soft muds.

Upon reaching the cove of the settling lake,
I stripped from the wash of these
threads and wait for the blaze of the morning sun.

Past the Crossing Bridge

The path to the crossing bridge caressed each stone and rock
rigged with mumbling vowels.

I speak of her with enhancement and
flickering gems of washing beads
which thread across the breasts of the opening sliver of driftwood
which I gathered in the swift snare of my palms.

I reach to her upon the grip of the kelp
held upon the sunken log deeply coiled with
this soot, reaching both channel
and the wedge of the reaching boulder by waters edge.

I turn and face the drip of this mountain stream as every hushing
breath of water falls upon the groove of the cascade and
trickling press of each curve.

Walking across each wooden plank,
I look to the nave of the sky and loosen
upon the breath of the winds
which scurry through each softened thread
of each cotton wrapped along
my shoulders and waist.

October's End

Into the evening of October, I breathed the
aromas of the rich, suckle of the earth.

Clouds lulled as a canvas, grooming the soft tremble of the trees;
softly, auburn leaves pampered upon my
shoulder, I reach to the flicker
of each twig and branch.

I stop by the motioning quiver of the creek.
gentle, I drank the freshest water from the iced drip and shook
upon the edged ferns which threaded along the softest brook.

Now, the last moment of October, I
listen to the 'caw' of the crows
which took flight and angled to the meadow.

I look upon the end of the farthest valley
and I witness white beds of snow
lulling in ivories and trees coated in alabaster branches.

The fog fell swift to the spread of the earth and I moaned for the
cottons to take me and fade across the
pinches of gathered cool grass.

Winter's Advance

The forest stretched as a guild for empty trees and naked buds
which quiver in the chill of Autumn's end.

This pampered woods of fallen leaves and
crackling smack of branches
exclaimed of their nakedness and Winter's advance.

I stopped and looked upon her as she lays
in a mound of red and auburn
leaf piles.

So eager, I trembled at the touch of her
lips; I breathed the pearl beads
alive on the crest of her breasts.

By nightfall, she dripped and faded through
the fall of the sweetest mist.

Spirits of the Woods

As I frequent these lusty woods, full and heavy
the rains melded with the earth and suckled
by the spread of these winding roots; each finger of the twitching ferns
dampen the tread of my boots and their tamp.

I turn my face and lean from the canvas of the treetops.

Sweet scents and flavors of mint tremble through me
as the fall of the pinecone relished upon the muds of the moaning
earth; I suckled the splash and wash as the rain peppered the ground.

I lasted the longevity of the descent of the strain of the Summer woods.

As the crimping leaves of Autumn gathered at the groove
of my feet, I filled my lungs with the fallen mist and threads
of each layer of fog.

Passages in the Autumn Hour

The angled edge of the wheat field pressed to the river, alive
in the speed and quickness of the gushing rapids which caressed
the rocks and kelp.

I unravelled from the groin of the earth and stood in nakedness;
softly, I walked in the press of the scurrying waters.

My flesh layered upon the harvest of the earth.

I sank to the rich moisture of these damp fields and I offer the curve
of my ribs and the mulch of my flesh as the distance of Winter
gnaws upon the crest of each marrow and fill of my bloods.

Winds tossed through the quiver of the wheat and I surrender
so close to the passages of the juices of the dancing river.

In the Morning You Perish

Your warm breath spread across my flesh, so tangled
in the crisp chill of this Autumn moan.

Sweetly, I placed my finger upon the paints of your lips
as the fall of the elm leaf traced across the curve of my shoulder
and slipped down the reach of my arms.

I opened my glazes upon the naked silks of my pearl swept neck
and clavicle.

You place your hands above the bloods of my skin.

Heat blooms upon my groin, cheeks and my face lathers
in the press of the flavor of harvest, the dance of my hair
twines with yours.

I awoke to the floods of emptiness as the scent of you dwindles
and perishes.

Tender Earth

From clifftop to adjacent cliff, the wood of the bridge
Spoke of the antiquity and the clever moss which stretched
And wrapped across the creaking planks.

I paused and witnessed the slight wave of the scattered trees
Which tossed and fumbled the leaf of the maple and the leaf
Of the sycamore which fondled the falling sky.

Evening hues of red and tan loafed by bridge
And scurried along the stream, slicing in rivets of the canal.

I walk into the heavy spread of the mumbling forest branches.
Quietly, I lose my way and eagerly, I suckle the roots and mulch
Which wraps each finger about me and I permeate the tender earth.

Grove

The flesh of the peach slipped across the basin of my mouth, tongue
and jaw.

Burrowing in the patterned grove, I lean against the leaves
which sauntered as eaves and rain patted the silence of the earth.

Now, crossing the threshold into the Autumn chill, I tremored
to the dance of the sky which coddled and lusted upon me.

Leaves flickered through the spiny, frosted grass and I suckled the
snap and gush
of the fallen fruits which wedge upon my throat.

Slouching into the dark sludge of the dome of heaven,
I fell in the slumber of these motioning trees which frequent
the starving soil and crust of the earth.

White Veils

At the end of Autumn, the iced fangs slouched and sank
to the fleece of the virgin earth, housing each spread of white
quilted beds of snow.

The trail rose to the graves of the meadow;
I listened and heard the voices and moans of the fellowship
which halted at the edge of the woodlands.

I paused and gazed upon the fullness of the oak tree
which stretched as a monarch across the floor of the meadow,
cloaked behind me in the cotton sheets of snowbeds,
full and tender.

In the patience of the swift shadow of the death
of each tree leaf in each patch within the woods,
I sank my boots with each give of the softest white veil
moaning across the winded pasture and forest yield.

Ivory Flank

The wind carved upon the shades and hues of green grass
and the roots which threaded, deep of the onion stalk.

The fullness of my hair took to the breeze of the red
sky, a dampening of the Autumn flash.

Sweet wavering gestures of the naked trees rattle to each
neighboring branch; the twig, filled with sap, molded
upon the breath of the heavy sky.

I stand and retrieve myself from the approaching ivory flank,
swarming across the depth of the northern gush.

Roots and bones beneath the soft, white gown of the covered earth
echoed their mangled, fading dusts;
I sweetly listen to the voices of her as the buds and pods
snap and scurry seeds, loafing upon the fumes and fog
treading across the carpets of the cakes of the earth.

So Near the Edge of Winter

The rain freshened and pampered across the stillness
of the motionless pond which carved the shape and precision
Of the curves of this edge, alive with the dampness of spreaded
leaves which curled and fell to the soils of the woods.

I listened to the moan of the empty, naked branches.
each branch of every tree whipped and crashed against
every adjacent tree.

There formed a glaze upon the slick moisture of each patch
of mud and gathering of the leaves of past October.

I entered upon the thickest stretch of the woods as I trembled
in the passage and swiftly I lost my way.

Ancient Graves

The trickling water gathered by the edge of the path
as the weeds suckled every dash, bead and pearl.

Skies dome stretched in dark hues of gray as the belly of the clouds
severed and empty itself of rain upon the softest earth.

In the fall of the gown of the heaven's trembling fog
which groomed and tugged each thickly buried root,
I stepped upon the heavy muds which coated the earth.

Slowly, I walked through the passage of the gnarled field;
tender, I spoke of supple coats of the meadow, once quivering
bones as they once shook, now grip the rigged roots
of the deepening, tender soil.

Autumn Nudity

I cross the threshold of Summer and step upon the sliver
and moment of Autumn.

I walk upon the slight dressing of painted trees
as each root of each towering branch, quivered and
spoke of my tamp upon the earth.

Slashes within the open gust of the gash where the spirited
winds danced upon me, I shook to the chill and frosted spread
over each thicket of greens.

I embrace the quiver of every pine and the floods upon the raised
press and hook of the risen root.

I embrace the shiver and slash, tenderly these rushing streams
covet the foamed and frothy water as sweet fangs of the fruit
tree fastens in and loosens, now, alive in the grasp
of Autumns nudity, quietly I awaken.

Travel

Wilted buds of the tree branch dispersed upon the ground,
So covered with leaves which trembled across the earth,
I breathed the fragrance of this heavy October groom;
sweet scents of the mints danced across me
with the gasp and bloom of the dusts which tossed through the sky,
close to the mumbling soil where I retreat.

Frost of the field of grass stings and burns the flesh of me as I
coddle the rhythms of this hymnal of Autumn night.

I undo the threads of my wool shirt and denim pants.
As
Reaching the slithering smash of the first shard of light
which tangled on the chill of Autumn
and the suns blazed through until the arms of supple Spring
coiled around my flesh and the toss of the fullness of my hair
and the sweat of my bust.

Travel

Wilted buds of the tree branch dispersed upon the ground,
So covered with leaves which trembled across the earth,
I breathed the fragrance of this heavy October groom;
sweet scents of the mints danced across me
with the gasp and bloom of the dusts which tossed through the sky,
close to the mumbling soil where I retreat.

Frost of the field of grass stings and burns the flesh of me as I coddle the rhythms of this hymnal of Autumn night.

I undo the threads of my wool shirt and denim pants.
I undo and pronounced myself to the secretions of every sap of the wood.

Reaching the slithering smash of the first shard of light
which tangled on the chill of Autumn
and the suns blazed through until the arms of supple Spring
coiled around my flesh and the toss of the fullness of my hair
and the sweat of my bust.

Empty Upon Return

Upon the bold, powders lofting from her soothing and free
Nakedness, I place my lips upon her saps and tangle into the torrents
Of each of her quaking thighs.

The dampness of each pearl bead resting upon her breasts,
I slither across her abdomen and summit of this flesh.

With the molten surrender of the red and pink of the sky,
I gathered my things and walk to the east with the apples
And figs, I slant beneath the press of the musk which lingers across me.

Further, into the deep of Autumn,
I return to the quilt of the trimmed grotto where once we rested.

I stand in the lone waves of the departed and I quiver as the growth
Of the edge of October stands empty before me.

Swallow of the Ocean Cove

I look to the loosely threaded clouds and
witnessed the curve of the sun
sleek upon a soft narrow path.

Quick and spirited, I swallowed the rains
as they tapped in sweet fragrance
of the nearest of mountain peaks.

With silence, now the slouching breath of
the ocean and the ocean cove,
I meld to the humid dance of the humid
drenching clouds, thinned
with the velvet scar of nightfall.

As Frost Fell Upon the Leaves on the Forest Floor

In the width of the open sky spoke to me of the caress
of the cool, chill which flooded the tall, narrow reach
of the emptiness of every crippling moan of the willow
and the birchwood.

Every flickering leaf swam to the floor of these heavy woods.

I filled myself with aromas of the past, weathered gems
across the forest earth, then, the deep of the Autumn shedding
branches where the sheets of linens lay lined with leaves.

I motioned my way to the rise of the sun.
Further to escape the setting quilt of night.

End of Winter at the Bones of This Burial

Walking in the beginning of the colored shards which glazed
across the damp leaves and the gasp of this smoky, humid breath.

I shuffled the steps of each foot and rose to the quiver
of each aroma, fallen in the sweet flavors of this pregnant earth.

I move to the angles of your flesh, tossed upon the nudity
where your sleek shadowed breasts unfurl and dance beneath
the voice of the shedding trees.

Together, we kneel by the stream and flourish juices and fullness
alive in the mountain stream.

Caught in the heaviest of snows, I lay upon you in linens
and sweetly, I wash each edge of your trembling bones
which quiver beneath the earth.

Road's End

I belong to the pale white snowbeds which wrestle upon the earth,
so filled with the rib of the soil and marrow which speaks of
all hidden antiquities.

I engulf the scents of the bloods of each caress of each fallen leaf.

Here, I swoon and grasp the bones in which I long to perish with,
fade in the blossoms of the veils of the wicker colored dress of linens.

~

I unravel to the fall of the sting where ices grip upon the arms
of the birchwood and stretch of the willow tree.

Held in the warmth of her fleshy arms and press of her
breasts, silent and trembling with cream,
I fade to the sour packaged
soils beneath. Calmly, I sleep in the quilted
array of leaves and branches.

I drink from the mountain creek as her shadow,

blooms across me.

About the Author

Donny Barilla, a poet covering the realms: human intimacy, nature, mythology, theology, and man's relationship with death and the departed, has been writing for over three decades. He writes daily and strives to renew himself as an artist from page to page and body of work to body of work. Very seldom does he take a break from writing as he views it as a full-time job. He lives a reclusive lifestyle and finds himself clinging close to nature and all her elements. His home state of Pennsylvania strikes chords of poetic depth about him as he finds loveliness from cornfield to meadow. Whether it's feelings of love, intimacy, or a special closeness, he maintains the feeling that death does not take these with him/her to the grave. Emotions and feeling outlast the flesh of the human body. Human intimacy draws near an enigmatic spiritual passion which conquers all on the prismatic scale of experience. When speaking of mythology Donny says, "myths were created to make sense of feelings which are complicated by very nature. They are perhaps more easily understood through persons greater than oneself. As for theology, a disciplined aspect, incorporates quite finely with passions and secured poetic comforts.
https://twitter.com/BarillaDonny

www.ingramcontent.com/pod-product-compliance
Lightning Source LLC
Chambersburg PA
CBHW032233080426
42735CB00008B/828